CW01083757

"The more that you read, t
things you will know. The
you learn, the more places you'll go." -
Dr. Seus

"In a world where you can be anything, be kind."

– Unknown

"You are never too old to set another goal or to dream a new dream." - C.S. Lewis

"Believe you can and you're halfway there." - Theodore Roosevelt

"No act of kindness, no matter how small, is ever wasted." – Aesop

"It's not what happens to you, but how you react to it that matters." – Epictetus

"Happiness is not something ready-made. It comes from your own actions."
- Dalai Lama

"It always seems impossible until it's done." - Nelson Mandela

"Sometimes the smallest things take up the most room in your heart." - A.A. Mil

"A person who never made a mistake never tried anything new." - Albert Einstein

"Don't watch the clock; do what it does. Keep going." - Sam Levenson

"You miss 100% of the shots you don't take." - Wayne Gretzky

"Every accomplishment starts with the decision to try." - John F. Kennedy

"Be yourself; everyone else is already taken." - Oscar Wilde

"Believe in yourself and all that you are.
Know that there is something inside you
that is greater than any obstacle." -
Christian D. Larson

"We do not remember days, we remember moments." - Cesare Pavese

"Don't let yesterday take up too much of today." - Will Rogers

"You are stronger than you seem, braver than you believe, and smarter than you think." - Christopher Robin

"The difference between ordinary and extraordinary is just that little extra." - Jimmy Johnson

"It's not what's under the Christmas tree that matters, it's who's around it." - Charlie Brown

"Don't be afraid to be different. Be afraid of being the same as everyone else." – Unknown

"Be curious, not judgmental." - Walt Whitman

"Success is not in what you have, but who you are." - Bo Bennett

"It's not about how fast you go. It's about enjoying the journey." – Unknown

"The best way to predict your future is
to create it." - Abraham Lincoln

"Darkness cannot drive out darkness; only light can do that. Hate cannot drive out hate; only love can do that." - Martin Luther King Jr.

"You are never too young to make a difference." - Greta Thunberg

"Don't be afraid to ask questions. Curiosity leads to knowledge." –
Unknown

"Hard work beats talent when talent doesn't work hard." - Tim Notke

Printed in Great Britain
by Amazon